SHEILA PETERSON

Awaken to the higher consciousness : THE CHAKRA BLISS

Unlock the secrets to a balanced life through a harmonious journey

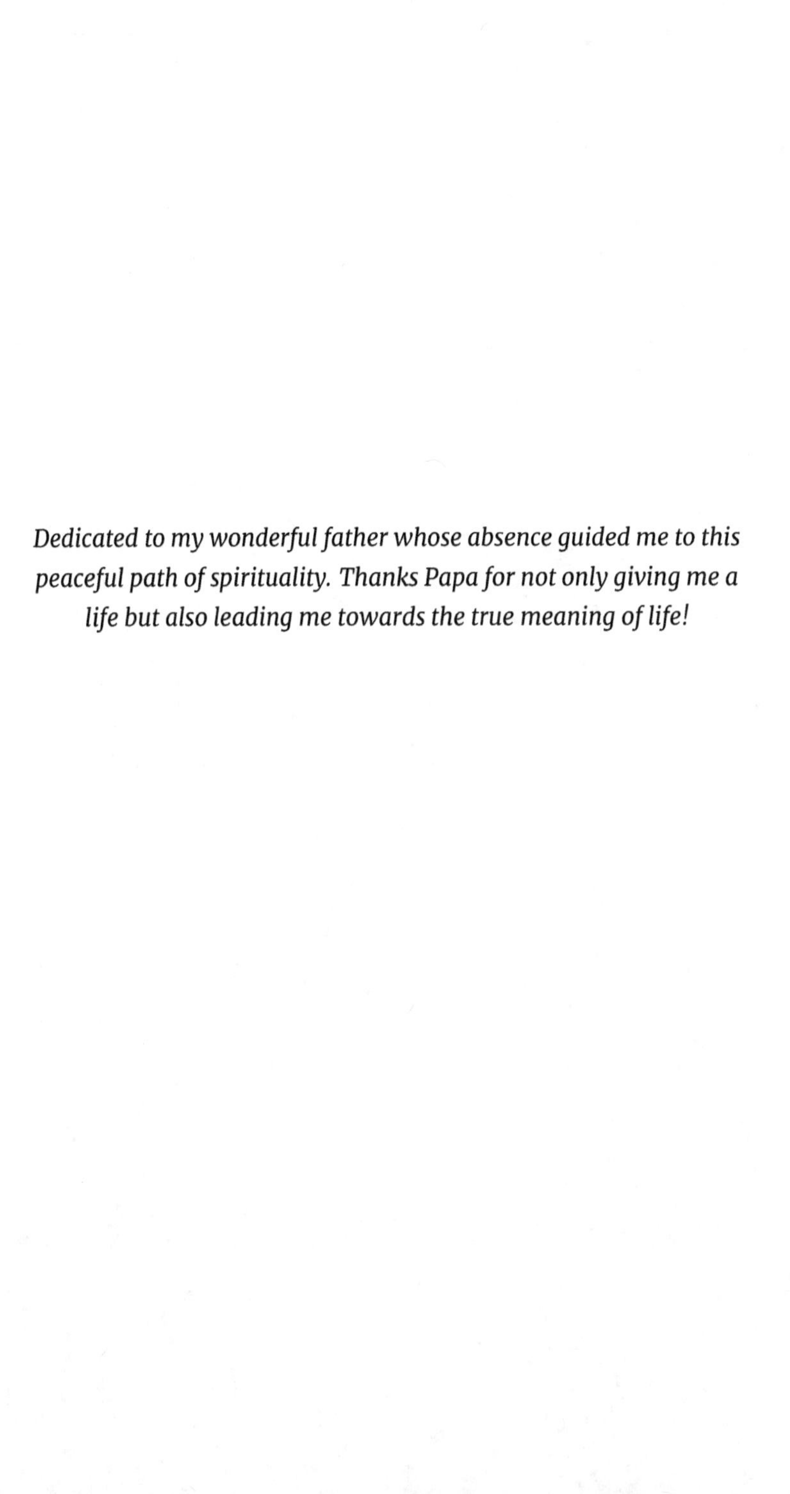

Dedicated to my wonderful father whose absence guided me to this peaceful path of spirituality. Thanks Papa for not only giving me a life but also leading me towards the true meaning of life!

Contents

1

Introduction

Being the regular householders, we often are unable to under-stand certain matters happening inside and around us. We all have wounds from our past to heal, wounds that bother us, pains that we are used to carrying along, such as traumas, phobias, physical ills, etc. In today's modern and busy world, it has become hard to take proper care of our minds and bodies. We have normalised so many feelings like anger, stress, competition, sadness, etc. that are actually harmful for the mankind. With a proper alignment of body and mind, man can actually live the life to the fullest. Let's understand, how the science of Chakras can help us align our mind, body and thoughts altogether and help us discover a perfect way to heal.

Through Asana practice, meditation and affirmations, one can stimulate and balance these chakras or energy centres in the body. As we move ahead, we will learn more about the 7 chakras, their symbols, attributes, effects, and balancing techniques. Some people say that chakras are one foot in radius, while others say that they change their size according to the energy flow.

Scriptures, on the other hand, tell us that the chakras are very small, as they are located in the astral spinal cord, which is further located inside the physical spinal cord. The focus of this book is chakras and their energy, which if opened and balanced, can bring numerous mental and physical healing effects on our everyday life.

This book will help you learn and discover some meditation and mindfulness techniques to have access to your inner-spirituality and enhance the ability to heal your mind and your spirit while cleansing your chakras.

2

How did it happen to me?

"If you want to lead a balanced life, you must nurture your inner self every now and then darling!" said a witty lady to me winking an eye with a smirk smile. While we exchanged a small talk around the topic, I realized that I was merely involved in that conversation as I was already worried about the upcoming events waiting for my attention back home- What's for dinner?, Who walked the dog today? Is the laundry done? Am I on track with my bills? Do I have enough savings for future? Have I already sent the meeting invitation to the department? Is my presentation ready or did I miss to add the performance chart for the recent quarter? and the list went on. In the background my heart was aching and I was profoundly missing my Dad. I had lost my Dad in the earlier month. As I was far away when he passed on, I couldn't see him for the last time. Since my childhood, he held a great impression on me and we were each other's favourites. Along with the time, I tried to move on. I pretended to feel normal at work and home but deep in my heart the pain of losing my Dad was always there.

It was my routine to visit this cafe after work. I used to sit around the window table and enjoy my coffee with a view. I just loved watching people rushing around their lives and kept wondering that as soon as I finished my coffee, I was going to be a part of that crowd. Suzan, the coffee shop owner and my witty friend, was well aware of my all thoughts. She would try to preach me in many ways and would say at last "You'll know everything in a blink, only when it's your time!" Little did I know how deep and thoughtful that was. And, it happened all suddenly.

As I logged into my computer and started dealing with each task robotically on a typical work day, an email flashed into my inbox. Well, my dues were paid, and I was asked to wrap up. Just like that! I was just a week away from finishing my probation period at this job, and now I was jobless already. In that particular moment, I wasn't sure if I was numb, senseless, sad, depressed or surprised at all. I couldn't react or ask for any valid reasons. I didn't defend myself at all. It made me sweat surely, but I didn't feel the heartbreak. Wow! Without investigating much further, I wrapped up my stuff like an obedient kid and boarded a cab to home. In that particular moment, I missed my Dad immensely. It came to my mind that today I had some extra time to visit my favourite coffee shop. So I decided to have a peaceful cup of coffee before heading to home. I sat at my regular table for some peace but my mind was racing faster towards the future and throwing all the unseen risks and worries at me. Suzan and I talked. At the end of our talk, she asked me what I really wanted? Honestly, I just wanted to be in the present moment, all the time and deal with the current situation instead of rushing into the future always. Suzan asked me to do a favor to myself. "Instead of finding another job immediately, spend a week or at least an hour a day with yourself.

Once you know who you are, you'll certainly find what do you want to do?" Suzan soothingly convinced me. Well, I guess, she had succeeded to motivate me to begin my journey.

The knowledge and awareness of chakras came to me. Legends say that things happen at the time they're supposed to happen. The knowledge has always been around but now was my time to learn and utilize it for my betterment. With the help of my Teacher, I not only learnt about the chakras but balanced my blockages, overcame my fears and shortcomings, rediscovered myself, and fell in love with this new me. And here, I'm sharing this learning with you. Let's begin with the basics.

What are chakras?

Chakras are basically the energy centres of the body that greatly impact our lives. We have physical body, subtle body or astral body, emotional body, causal body and spiritual body. The chakras form a part of our subtle body. The chakras in our subtle body beautifully cross over the endocrine system. They coincide with the adrenal glands. They are located along the spine, starting at its base and running upwards to the crown of the head. The astral body is the energy body residing inside our physical body. The astral body cannot be seen or touched. This is also a reason why we cannot see the chakras. In simple words, if you cut open a human body, you won't be seeing the energy illuminating chakras with a special effect! There are total 114 chakras in our subtle body out of which 7 are the most prominent ones. The chakras radiate a specific colour and energy. Each one coincides with a gland in the physical body. Since each chakra relates to specific spiritual, emotional, psychological, and physical aspects of our being, it is believed that their blockage or malfunction can lead to physical, psychological, and emotional disorders. The conscious awareness and balancing of these energy centres, on the other hand, is believed to lead to well-being and good health.

All human beings are energies. We absorb and emit the energies constantly. We all are potentially divine beings and we are naturally spiritually inclined. We are born with this divine energy but as we grow and go through the materialistic life, we develop our mind-ego. This hidden ego keeps telling us about the insufficiencies and develops insecurities about our existence in many ways. Many people end up feeling bad for their appearance, colour, lifestyle or work. We experience good and bad all time. With balanced chakras and energy, we can assess the situations in much better ways and develop the ability deal with all situations without it letting overpower us.

Can Chakras influence health?

Chakras are associated with the organs and glands of the particular region where they are located. As such, they have a strong bearing on our health, our mental state,andour relation with others. Based on various factors such as our lifestyle, environment and surroundings, past experiences, etc, the chakras can either be balancedor imbalanced.If a chakra is imbalanced, it goes into either a hypoactive or a hyperactive mode. A hypoactive or blocked chakra's functioning is either insufficient or reduced. Likewise, a hyperactive chakra means there is too much energy flowing into that particular region, and as such, there is an imbalance in the overall flow of energy throughout the body.

How do I know if my Chakras are blocked?

Since chakras are interrelated, when one of them is imbalanced, it causes a disturbance in the functionality of the other chakras as well. This makes people feel disconnected, anxious, fearful, and it also manifests as health problems in one or more areas of the body.

To function at their best,your chakras need to be balanced. And for this, you need to know what the chakras actually do and what are some of the things you can do to take care of them.

How to balance your Chakras?

Every chakra rotates at a specific frequency and speed. This frequency and speed can change due to various factors like diet, lifestyle, thought patterns, etc. An imbalance starts creating problems with the distribution of the life forces. Imagine what will happen if a 50 watt light bulb starts getting a 500 watt or 10-watt electricity supply! When we speak about balancing or awakening the chakras, we mean bringing them back to their regular speed.

There is no one single method to unblock your chakras, but rather several. The best way to unblock your chakras will be different for everyone. Here are a few popular tools and techniques for chakra cleansing and balancing:

1. *Diet*

One of the main reasons for an imbalance in the chakras is

an imbalance of the five elements in the body. A balanced diet helps to bring balance to the elements of the body.

2. Asanas

Asanas help to stimulate the chakras, and improve their functioning. They also clear the way for the chakras to heal themselves.

3. Breathing exercises

Breathing helps to increase the flow of prana in the body, and removes the stale prana.

4. Meditation

Many practitioners perform meditation to unblock chakras. Chakra meditation calms the mind and helps the practitioner focus energy towards a problematic point in the chakra system.

5. Mudras

Mudras are hand gestures typically performed in yoga and meditation to focus energy where it's needed most. To balance the chakras, we balance the element in the body by performing the corresponding mudra.

3

Chapter-1: Root Chakra

The Root chakra is the base chakra. As the name suggests, it is located at the base of the spine, in the perineum area. To understand the physical location, just focus on the part of the body that touches the ground when you sit cross legged on the ground or floor. It is characterized by the emotions of survival, stability, ambition, and self-sufficiency. This chakra also stores your past life deeds and is responsible for your strong or weak base. It literally acts as the roots of a tree, holding your base in the ground and giving you support to grow higher out in the world. Let's try to understand this concept with an example of a plant. We provide water, soil and manure in the roots to nurture a plant. The roots absorb everything and the plant grows. Similarly, your thoughts, deeds and actions get absorbed in your Root chakra and reside there through your journey. Little do you notice that they shape your very existence and current experiences. Now, you might be getting an idea how a weak Root chakra could affect one in real life!

The element of the Root chakra is Earth. The human body is made of 5 elements out of which the earth element is dominant.

Legends say that we come from the soil and become soil one day. As long as we are breathing, we exist. The moment the life force moves out from the body, we eventually decay and become a part of the earth. Hence, our connection with the mother Earth actually helps understand the state of our Root chakra.

Symbol

The Root Chakra symbol consists of a 4-petalled lotus flower, a square, and a downward-facing triangle. Each element is said to represent the 4 aspects of the human mind, uniting to form the birth of the human consciousness.

Symptoms of a blocked/imbalanced Root Chakra

When this chakra is out of balance, a person starts feeling unstable, ungrounded, lack of ambition, lack of purpose, lack of commitment, fearful, insecure and frustrated. An unbalanced Root chakra could influence a person's personal, social and professional relationships.

Signs of a balanced Root Chakra

However, when the Root Chakra is balanced, the insecurities

are replaced by more positive emotions, and one feels stable, confident, balanced, energetic, independent, and strong. They tend to react to matters more responsively resulting in wonderful outputs.

How to balance the Root chakra?

As we have learnt that the Root chakra is associated with the mother Earth, we need to connect with the mother Earth as much as possible. We are used to wear footwear all the times. So for starters, try to walk bare foot on the ground. It is not necessary to get up and walk on the grass immediately. Well if you can, it's a blessing, trust me. But even if you are able to walk on the floor for a while without footwears, you can feel the connection with the ground. Taking care of the greenery around, spending time around plants, trees and nature is a great remedy for this chakra. The day you work on your Root chakra, try to spend some time in your plants nursery, if you have access to one. Watering plants and cleaning the soil can actually help you connect with earth. It is observed that people living in the countryside or at villages have stronger Root chakra as they are closer to the mother Earth and nature than the city folks.

Food to strengthen the Root chakra

The colour of this chakra is Red. When working on your Root chakra, you can focus on eating the food that we yield from mother Earth or ground like root vegetables, onions, potatoes, carrots, ginger, beet root, sweet potatoes etc.

Body part associated with the Root chakra

The physical organ associated with this chakra is nose. Activating your smelling senses can ease your Root chakra. Try to smell flowers and soft essences. You may try burning scented candles or essence sticks at home. While bathing, try using soothing bathing oil drops once a while.

Mantra and posture for the Root chakra

The seed mantra (one word mantra) of the Root Chakra is 'Lam.' When you seat in a quiet place, take a deep breath in and while exhaling slowly chant 'Lam.' If possible, you may hold the Earth posture while doing this. Rest your palms on your thighs facing the sky/ceiling (assuming you are seated crossed legged on the ground or mat) and touch the tips of the thumb and the ring finger, holding the rest finger straight.

Yoga poses/Aasanas to balance the Root Chakra

1. Tree Pose
2. Mountain Pose
3. Warrior Pose
4. Chair Pose
5. Yogic Squat
6. Standing Forward Bend

4

Chapter-2: Sacral Chakra

The Sacral chakra is also known as the Womb chakra. It is located in the lower abdomen, about four fingers below the navel. We all begin our lives in our mother's womb, and that's where this chakra is developed. It is utterly important to heal this chakra as the solutions to the 80% of your life problems lie here in this chakra. It is a very powerful and energetic point in your body as it holds a key to tremendous healing. It can mend the broken relationships and clear negativity. The karmic trauma and residues from all our past journeys are stored in our Root and Sacral chakras.

Its attributes include the basic need for sexuality, reproduction, as well as creativity and self-worth. The lower abdominal area where this chakra resides, acts as an important part of our human body as our reproduction organs are located here. Each human being hosts dual energies- masculine and feminine, irrespective of the gender. This chakra holds the emotions that are carried forward from the donors to the new life that shapes up in the womb. Hence, from a healthy and happy pregnancy, a healthy life form is born whereas an uncherished conceiving and carrying may result into an emotionally and physically weak life form. A women goes through a lot of emotional, hormonal and physical changes during her pregnancy. And these all changes, along with the environmental changes around her social circle get absorbed in the new life inside her. In simple words, the Sacral chakra influences the thoughts, energies and emotions of the mother on the sacral chakra of the new creation. This chakra is also responsible for our creative side. So when you feel blocked at work, not getting new ideas, missing the creativity in life/relationships or feeling left out, work on your Sacral chakra.

Symbol

The symbol for the Sacral Chakra is made up of multiple circles, a crescent moon, and six lotus flower petals. The circles and crescent moon represent the cyclical nature of life, death, and rebirth, while the 6 petals portray the 6 negative aspects of our nature that we need to overcome to open this chakra.

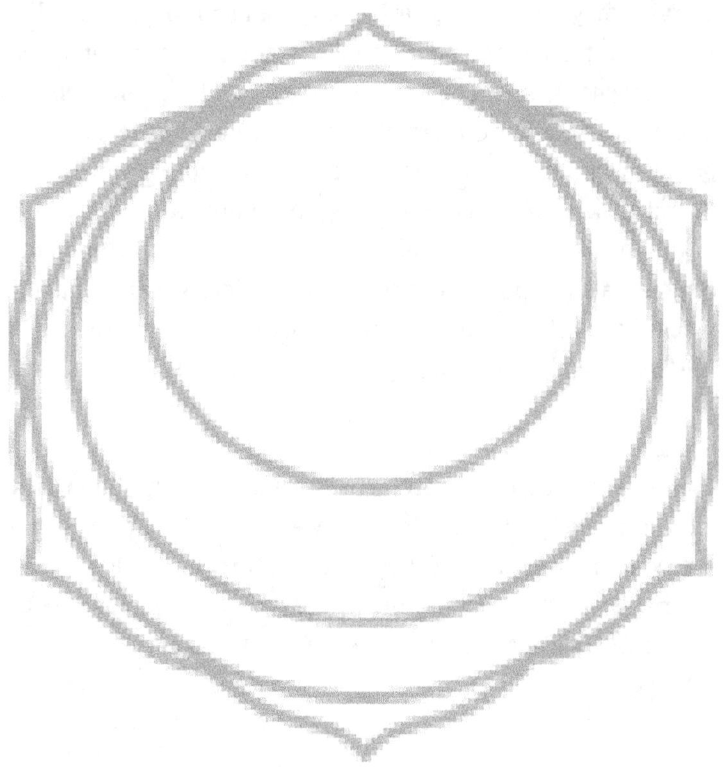

Symptoms of a blocked/imbalanced Sacral Chakra

When the Sacral Chakra is imbalanced, a person may feel emotionally explosive and irritable, sense a lack of energy and creativity, feel manipulative, or obsessed with sexual thoughts. Any form of addiction might be a result of an imbalanced Sacral chakra. Hormonal imbalance is measuredly caused by this chakra. An imbalanced Sacral chakra might affect a person's social and family life. The lack of creativity can influence one's academic or professional side as well. If someone experiences any unresolved emotional cliches with their mother, it is highly recommended to work on their Sacral chakra and break the vicious cycle.

Signs of a balanced Sacral Chakra

When balanced, it makes one feel more vibrant, happy, friendly, optimistic, positive, satisfied, compassionate, and intuitive. One can find alignment with their thoughts and actions at personal as well as professional levels. A person with a balanced Sacral chakra will experience harmony and security in relationships and can naturally be happy in their own skin. There's no room for emotions like jealousy and insecurity.

How to balance the Sacral chakra?

The element of the Sacral chakra is water which also is an important element out of the 5 elements that our body comprises of. Spending time around water bodies works miraculously with an imbalanced Sacral chakra. Taking a stroll along beachside or walking peacefully by a lakeside helps a lot to settle the inner disturbance. However, not each of us gets a luxury to live around water bodies in a practical life. So here's a workaround and a practical solution that most of us can surely afford. Try taking a long bath, invest in a leisure bath once in a while, spend some extra time in the bath tub or under the shower and while doing so observe the water touching and passing through your body. Instead of having just a mechanical shower, get involved in the process and with the water feelings. Occasionally, buy some nice bath salts, candles, and any other accessories that might relax you. Listening to the sound of water or waterfalls can also help. It is observed that people living around coast side, sea shore, or around water bodies lead a satisfactory and peaceful life.

Food to strengthen the Sacral chakra

The colour of the Sacral chakra is orange. When working on an imbalanced Sacral chakra you can focus on eating food like pumpkin, carrots, honey, apricots, oranges, etc.

Body part associated with the Sacral chakra

The physical organs associated with this chakra are reproduction system (both male and female) and kidneys. Balancing your hormones, having healthy reproductive system, having healthy and well-functioning kidneys can ease your Sacral chakra. Managing the water intake and keeping body well hydrated can also help in many ways.

Mantra and posture for the Sacral chakra

The seed mantra (one word mantra) of the Sacral Chakra is 'Vam.' When you seat in a quiet place, take a deep breath in and while exhaling slowly chant 'Vam.' If possible, rest your palms on your thighs facing the sky/ceiling (assuming you are seated crossed legged on the ground or mat) and touch the tips of the thumb and the index finger, holding the rest finger straight.

Yoga poses/Aasanas to balance the Sacral Chakra

As this chakra resides in the pelvic area, hip opening poses work magically here. As an additional bonus, these poses aid an emotional release as well.

1. Triangle Pose
2. Goddess Pose
3. Butterfly Pose
4. Pigeon Pose
5. Happy child Pose

5

Chapter-3: Jewel Chakra or Solar Plexus Chakra

The Jewel chakra as the name itself suggests is the precious jewel that holds the important aspects of our physical existence. Knowing your own Jewel chakra opens one of the many possibilities to know yourselves in and out truly. If you understand this chakra and can focus on your naval centre, you can understand the entire cosmos. The Jewel chakra is located at the solar plexus, between the navel and the bottom of the rib cage. It is characterized by emotions like ego, anger, and aggression.

Your naval point is a spot of extreme spiritual significance. It is as important as the Sun in the galaxy. In absence of this chakra, mucus will rise in your body. It governs the fire element in your body and manages the acidity level. This chakra holds your very first pain memory, your umbilical cord being cut from placenta and being separated from your mother. Being a foetus in the womb, you are connected with the external world only through your naval point.

When you get an emotional churn or a feeling of excitement, you get butterflies in stomach, since a disturbed Jewel chakra is responsible for these feelings. Now you understand why they call the strong feelings as the gut feelings. You are very assure and positive about our gut feelings because they rise from your active Jewel chakra.

Symbol

The Jewel or the Solar Plexus chakra symbol consists of a downward-pointing triangle within a ten-petalled lotus flower. The ten petals symbolize ten negative character traits that we have to conquer, while the triangle is the Fire element energy which signifies our inner strength.

Symptoms of a blocked/imbalanced Jewel chakra

An imbalance of the Jewel Chakra can manifest physically as digestive problems, liver problems, excessive weight gain/loss, or diabetes. On an emotional level, one might struggle with depression, lack of self-esteem, anger, and perfectionism. Feeling dominated, ignored, left out or side lined in a relationship is a sign of a weak Jewel chakra. The tendency with an obsession to achieve perfection in every minor detail and to expect the same from the world around is also a result of an over active

Jewel chakra. Such behaviour can cost a person their social and professional relationships.

Signs of a balanced Jewel chakra

When balanced, this chakra makes one feel more energetic, confident, productive, and focused. A person with a well-balanced Jewel chakra can experience healthy gut, a well working digestive fire, good health, and energetic and active life style. It also signifies with a sense of security and good intuitive feelings.

How to balance the Jewel chakra

This chakra is connected with your naval point and hence deep breathing (through naval point) proves of immense benefit while working on this chakra. To activate the naval breathing, breath in deep and push the tummy out. Now, while breathing out release the air slowly and pull the tummy in. This way the lungs get a proper supply of oxygen. The ancient sciences say that the root of most of our health issues lies in the imbalanced digestive system. An imbalanced digestive fire is the result of an imbalanced Jewel chakra. If this chakra is not working optimally, no fancy diets or medicines can do their miracles up to their potential. A balanced Jewel chakra helps in internal correction of impurities.

Food to strengthen the Jewel chakra

The colour of the Jewel chakra is yellow. When working on an imbalanced Jewel chakra you can focus on eating food and spices that generate heat in body like mustard, asafoetida, sesame, papaya, etc.

Body part associated with the Jewel chakra

The physical organ associated with this chakra is digestive system. Balancing your digestive fire and gut health can ease your Jewel chakra. Instead of multitasking and being distracted while eating, paying full attention to the food and having a respectful schedule for meals can help balance the Jewel chakra.

Mantra and posture for the Jewel chakra

The seed mantra (one word mantra) of the Jewel Chakra is 'Ram.' When you seat in a quiet place, take a deep breath in and while exhaling slowly chant 'Ram.' If possible, rest your palms on your thighs facing the sky/ceiling (assuming you are seated crossed legged on the ground or mat) and touch the tips of the thumb and the index finger, holding the rest finger straight.

Yoga poses/Aasanas to balance the Jewel Chakra

All twisting poses are effective in activating the Jewel chakra. All the poses in the Sun salutations prove effectively beneficial while working on the Jewel chakra.

1. Frog Pose
2. Forward Bend
3. Cat and Cow Pose
4. Seated Fish pose or Half spinal twist
5. Boat pose

6

Chapter-4: Heart Chakra

As the name implies, the Heart chakra is located in the heart/chest region. This chakra is the seat of balance, and it is characterized by emotions of love, attachment, compassion, trust, and passion. Some deeply rooted emotions like grief or rejection are also connected with the Heart chakra. When we experience a loss of a loved one or a deeply connected relationship, our Heart chakra goes for a toss and hence we face difficulties in coping up with the situations around. The Heart chakra is an unstruck sound within us. A person's Heart chakra is said to be open when they are able to connect with their inner sound. This chakra is a place where one resides without any filters, the true self. This centre operates on love however it heals the deepest griefs. It is a bridge that connects you with the spiritual world and takes you towards your higher self. It awakens the humanity inside you and takes you to the divinity. This chakra gives you the power to discriminate between right and wrong. The element of this chakra is air.

Symbol

In the Heart Chakra symbol, two triangles intersect to form a design which represents the balance of yin and yang, or upward and downward forces. Outside, there is a lotus flower with 12 petals symbolizing the twelve divine qualities associated with the heart.

Symptoms of a blocked/imbalanced Heart chakra

When the heart chakra is imbalanced, a person may deal with emotional issues like anger, lack of trust, grief, rejection, anxiety, jealousy, fear, and moodiness. An overactive or underactive Heart chakra is also treated as an imbalanced one. In case of an overactive Heart chakra a person may react with extreme emotional sensitivity. On the contrary, under the influence of an underactive Heart chakra a person may find it challenging to overcome emotional blockages and may prefer living in denial instead of confronting the situation. Shyness, commitment issues, dwelling in the past could be the outcomes of an underactive Heart chakra.

Signs of a balanced Heart chakra

When balanced, this chakra makes one feel more caring, optimistic, friendly, and motivated. This chakra enables you to develop deep, mature, and meaningful relationships with others. By harmonizing this energy centre, a person begins to feel more connected and compassionate and can easily bond with others. A person with a well-balanced Heart chakra can experience peace even in shattered or difficult times. With a balanced personality, a person can accept others for their true selves, including their flaws and without a judgemental attitude.

How to balance the Heart chakra

Meditation is the best approach when dealing with an imbalanced or underactive Heart chakra. Breathing exercises such as equal breathing and breath balancing also prove miraculous in healing the Heart chakra. When meditating (with closed eyes), sit straight with erected spine, try to focus on the centre of the eyebrows and pay attention to your breath movement. Slowing down the thought process can ease your mind and sooth your heart. The meditative practices help you to deal with loss or pain and to move on.

Body part associated with the Heart chakra

The physical organs associated with this chakra are heart, lungs, and shoulders.

Mantra and posture for the Heart chakra

The seed mantra (one word mantra) of the Heart Chakra is 'Yam.' When you seat in a quiet place, take a deep breath in and while exhaling slowly chant 'Ram.' If possible, rest your palms on your thighs facing the sky/ceiling (assuming you are seated crossed legged on the ground or mat) and touch the tips of the thumb and the index finger, holding the rest finger straight.

Yoga poses/Aasanas to balance the Heart Chakra

All chest and shoulder opening stretches and poses help in opening the Heart chakra.

1. Bridge Pose
2. Half Bridge Pose
3. Camel Pose
4. Cobra Pose
5. Fish Pose

7

Chapter-5: Throat Chakra

Our divinity begins at the Throat chakra. As we saw earlier, the Heart chakra is a bridge between the materialistic and spiritual experiences. It connects both worlds. Once balanced, our journey towards the higher being begins at the Throat chakra. The Throat Chakra is located at the base of the throat, coinciding with the Thyroid gland. It is associated with inspiration, healthy expression, faith and the ability to communicate well. The true nature of a soul is to be happy, compassionate and being blissful. This chakra identifies your ability to express yourself in the outside world. In a conversation it is very important how and what we talk and receive. The speech delivery holds a great importance. The way the words are delivered determines the success or failure of the conversation. It is very important to know the barriers about the audiences and keeping conversation creative.

This chakra directly affects the Thyroid gland. It is also responsible for frequent occurrences of throat diseases like throat infections, sore throat, runny nose, etc. We all know what we consume, be it any food or thoughts, affects our well-being sensibly. The chakras are located in our energy body. Hence, anything that affects our energy body can strongly impact and imbalance this chakra as well. The element of the Throat chakra is space.

Symbol

The symbol of the Throat Chakra consists of a 16-petalled lotus flower surrounding an inverted triangle which holds a circle within. This represents spiritual growth and the purification of the body, mind, and spirit.

Symptoms of a blocked/imbalanced Throat Chakra: A blockage in the throat chakra may be experienced as timidity, quietness, a feeling of weakness, or the inability to express our thoughts. Preparing everything well in head but being hesitant or unable to express it, is commonly observed with an imbalanced Throat chakra. Even when speaking, many a times a person's thoughts are not aligned with the words or the context. Under the influence of an underactive Throat chakra, a person may adapt a tendency towards dishonesty, speaking lies, avoiding tasks, or taking shortcuts. This could result in further weakening of the Throat chakra.

With an overactive Throat chakra, a person may appear authoritative, not listening to the truth, or stressing over self-perspective only. Such people may seem to have confidence while talking but may not always be good listeners or conversationists. Sometimes an overactive Throat chakra may result in person's irrelevant or insensitive talking.

Signs of a balanced Throat Chakra: When this chakra is balanced, it enables creativity, positive self-expression, constructive communication, and a sense of satisfaction. A person with an established Throat chakra can get a strong hold on his/her audience. While delivering speech, their pause also catches a rhythm and is meaningful. A balanced Throat chakra also signifies with good listening qualities. A good listener leads in healthy conversations. They ask prompt and relevant questions. With a balanced Throat chakra, a person develops a healthy sense about correct audience and correct time. They share only the right content with the right audience instead of talking everything to everyone. Thus they make conversations comfortable for others as well. Some people are naturally gifted orators. Without any formal trainings or educations, they can give speeches with a great confidence and without hesitation. This is because their Throat chakra is well balanced.

How to balance the Throat chakra

When trying to work on your Throat chakra, try to be mindful in each talk. Focus on speaking truth but in a gentle manner and without hurting anyone's feelings directly. Maintaining a journal for yourself can also help as you can express your thoughts without hesitation. Listening to the birds chirping or the soothing sounds in the nature that we usually don't pay attention to can really help in improving the listening skills. This chakra is connected with your Thyroid gland point and hence breathing exercises associated with throat (such as Ujjayi breathing) prove of immense benefit while working on this chakra.

Body part associated with the Throat chakra

The physical organs associated with this chakra is throat.

Mantra and posture for the Throat chakra

The seed mantra (one word mantra) of the Throat Chakra is 'Ham.' When you seat in a quiet place, take a deep breath in and while exhaling slowly chant 'Ram.' If possible, rest your palms on your thighs facing the sky/ceiling (assuming you are seated crossed legged on the ground or mat) and touch the tips of the thumb and the index finger, holding the rest finger straight.

Yoga poses/Aasanas to balance the Throat Chakra

1. All neck rotation and neck flexing poses help in opening

the Throat chakra.

2. Throat Chakra is stimulated in poses like
3. Shoulderstand pose
4. Plough pose
5. Cat and Cow pose

8

Chapter -6: The Third Eye Chakra

The Third Eye Chakra is known as the seat of your intuitions and consciousness. This is where your higher-self resides. It is located between the eyebrows. It is often used as a focal point during meditation practices to develop more concentration and awareness. It has mystical abilities. This chakra corresponds to the pineal gland. This gland has a great impact on your physical and mental health. It secretes melatonin and serotonin and helps to set your biological body clock. When you tend to wake up every day at the same time without any alarms or triggers and fall asleep the time everyday naturally, it could be an indication of your Third Eye chakra being in place.

The Third Eye spot is a dormant spot as we are not very much aware about it always. Though, it is watching us in and out by watching our thoughts constantly. It is said that meditating upon this chakra destroys negative energies and brings liberation and intuitive knowledge. Its attributes are intelligence, intuition, insight, and self-knowledge.

Symbol

The Third Eye Chakra symbol consists of an inverted triangle resting in a circle between two lotus petals. The two petals and downward-facing pyramid both signify wisdom, emphasizing the Third Eye Chakra's role in our journey to spiritual awareness.

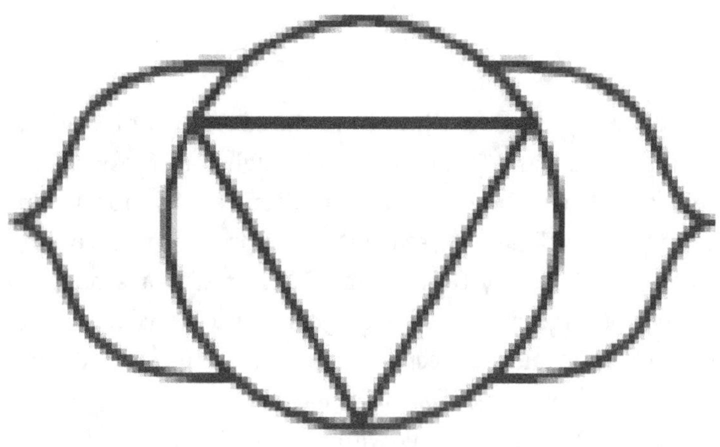

Symptoms of a blocked/imbalanced Third Eye Chakra: When imbalanced, this chakra may make you feel non-assertive and afraid of success, or on the contrary, it can make you more egotistical. An imbalance can manifest as physical problems like headaches, blurry vision, eye strain, and insomnia. An imbalanced Third Eye chakra may also cause lack of imagination, lack of visualisation and depression. When not balanced in time, a person's mental health may go for a toss for a while.

Signs of a balanced Third Eye Chakra: When this chakra is active and balanced, a person feels more vibrant and confident, both spiritually and emotionally. In the absence of the fear of death, one becomes his own master and remains free of all attachment to material things. A balanced Third Eye chakra also signifies the rise in imagination power and ability to decode the hidden messages from higher self. A person with a balanced Third Eye chakra can sync with the universe effortlessly. They eat consciously and always choose what is good and comfortable for them. As these people are in internally illuminated, they may feel sensitive to bright light and loud sound.

How to balance The Third Eye chakra

The Third Eye chakra is located between the eyebrows. Hence, pressing lightly with a finger between the eyebrows with closed eyes can help focus on the meditative point. As this chakra is sensitive to light, dimming the strong lights/lamps in the evening can offer a soothing effect. Before bedtime, keeping phones or any electronic gadgets away can not only strengthen the Third Eye chakra but also help you attain a naturally peaceful sleep. Eye exercises such as movement of eyeballs in specific manner give many benefits along with vision strengthening. Candle gazing proves immensely powerful while working with the Third Eye chakra.

Mantra

The seed mantra (one word mantra) of the Third Eye Chakra is 'Om'. When you seat in a quiet place, take a deep breath in and while exhaling slowly chant 'Ram.' If possible, rest your palms on your thighs facing the sky/ceiling (assuming you are seated crossed legged on the ground or mat) and touch the tips of the thumb and the index finger, holding the rest finger straight.

Yoga poses to balance the Third Eye Chakra

The Third Eye chakra is stimulated when practicing Head-stand.

9

Chapter -7: Crown Chakra

The Crown Chakra is located at the crown of the head. This seventh chakra is the centre of spirituality, enlightenment, and dynamic thought and energy. It allows for the inward flow of wisdom and brings the gift of cosmic consciousness. This is the last chakra to get active. With other chakras in place when you attain higher states of meditation, this chakra opens. It is said that it opens as if a thousand pious lotuses blooming together. It brings oneness within the practitioner and the world. This chakra is representation of wisdom and awareness. When this chakra is active, you are guided by higher power.

Symbol

The Crown Chakra symbol is depicted as a ring of a thousand lotus petals surrounding an inverted triangle. This symbolizes the rising of divine energy into the Crown Chakra, bringing spiritual liberation and enlightenment.

Symptoms of a blocked/imbalanced Crown Chakra: When it gets imbalanced, one might suffer from a constant sense of frustration, melancholy and destructive feelings. It could also manifest physical illnesses like headaches and eye problems. Under the influence of an imbalanced Crown chakra a person may have uncertain thoughts, tendency to dwell in past or roam in future, uncertainty about present, rigid beliefs, resistance to change. Fatigue and mental issues like stress and hallucination can also be the outcomes of an imbalanced Crown chakra.

Signs of a balanced Crown Chakra: A balanced Crown Chakra promotes spiritual understanding, inner peace and a clear perspective on the world. With a balanced Crown chakra the world appears as a part of yourself and not as a separate entity. You naturally treat everything and everyone with compassion and love. A person with a balanced Crown chakra attains his/her duties with moral awareness and is always is in spiritually awakened state. They develop a natural quality to put unwavering faith in everything the they do and everything that happens to them.

How to balance the Crown chakra

Your Crown chakra is in balanced state when you feel aligned internally without any distractions. Fasting and detoxing are a few practices that can help you gain physical lightness so you can more actively focus on your spiritual practices. Depending on your level and requirement you can opt for water fast, juice fast or one meal a day. Refraining from anger, bad or provoking thoughts also support to strengthen this chakra. The feeling of being lighter inside out enables to activate inner awareness. Cutting off from the external world for a while and focusing on your prayers and meditations energises your Crown chakra.

Mantra

The seed mantra (one word mantra) of Crown chakra is 'Aum'. When you seat in a quiet place, take a deep breath in and while exhaling slowly chant 'Ram.' If possible, rest your palms on your thighs facing the sky/ceiling (assuming you are seated crossed legged on the ground or mat) and touch the tips of the thumb and the index finger, holding the rest finger straight.

Yoga poses to align the Crown Chakra

Balancing Crown chakra can be done by practicing Headstand. Deep and focused meditations also help you elevate the state of mind.

10

Resources

Arhanta Yoga Ashrams. (2023, December 12). *Yoga teacher training online courses – Arhanta Yoga Ashrams.* https://www.arhantayoga.org/

Google. (n.d.). https://www.google.com/

11

Final Thought

The 7 chakras are powerful points in the energy body that help you maintain a healthy physical and emotional balance in life. For this reason, it's vital that you observe these energy centres regularly and take time out of your busy day to improve the flow of life to each. On a deeper level, aligning your chakras can also help you tune into your true Self and unlock the divine power within.

Leave a review comment to let me know your feedback about this book.